**Blues in
the Park**

by the same author

33 Poems (Sidgwick and Jackson)
Poems Out of Israel (Turret Books)
In Focus (Allison and Busby)

as editor

The Young British Poets (Chatto and Windus)
Poems from Poetry and Jazz in Concert (Souvenir Press)
Corgi Modern Poets in Focus (Vols 2 and 4)
Poetry Dimension 1 (Abacus)

For Olivia,
Valued friend and
colleague who keeps me
on the right path (some time!)

Love

Jeremy

Oct 17th
2014

**Blues in
the Park**
Jeremy Robson

SmOke
STACK
BOOKS

Smokestack Books
PO Box 408, Middlesbrough TS5 6WA
e-mail: info@smokestack-books.co.uk
www.smokestack-books.co.uk

Blues in the Park

Cover image: Leonid Afremov, *Winter Dream*
Author photo: Manuela Robson

ISBN 978-0-9927409-4-8

Smokestack Books is represented
by Inpress Ltd

for Carole, always

I know what I like
and what I like is you.

No need for tricky meters
or fancy rhymes, no need
for artifice or guile, to use
large brush strokes, startling
colours, adopt an ornate style.

It's always been that clear.
And though the years have brought
their testing times, for you, for me,
they've brought their treasures too
incalculable and true.

I know what I like
and no-one else will do.

Contents

Now and Then

I had opinions then on
many things, strongly felt, or
so I thought, and springing hotly
from the tongue, unsought.
But whose they were, and what the cost
and why they meant so much
is long since lost.

Now looking back, unmasked,
and as the ruthless years
exact their daily toll, it's
hard to know what role to play,
whose side to take, what cause
is just, what's really asked.

The eternal so-called truths
confuse the head, and mostly
are, I must confess, long dead.
I'd like to think that sure
but fading voice that now
sounds fake belonged to
someone else, a someone
on the make. But I can't
discard it quite, not yet,
though many of the 'wrongs'
I railed about seem right,
and many 'rights' scream wrong.

Holding back on different
fronts, diffident, less blindly sure,
may seem a coward's stance –
but not to me, with those years spent,
knowing now the voice that speaks
at least, at last, is mine, having
absorbed the bitter rules of time.

Final Set

I have to say
the serves aren't what
they were, the lobs
fall short, the drives
that grazed the lines
now dent the net.
The volley's limp, inept.

There must be easier
games than this,
where finesse and guile and
grey-haired wisdom score.
I need to change my style,
get off the floor.

The tight-jeaned girl
who meets my Romeo eye
on the Underground home
offers up her seat. That puts
me in my place! Depletes.

Still, I'll not give way,
may have to cheat, serve underarm,
up the pace, spin, call 'out'
when balls fall in.
It's not much fun, but no regrets,
I've had a decent run.

Back on court and serving
for the set, I swing
it wide, my favourite ploy –
it's back at twice the pace,
no ace, no joy. Can't win.

Time to bow out, that's
clear, but not without a shout.
'That shot, the one
you're calling good, you're wrong
the ball was inches long,
not even near.'

My set, my match, my day.
Applause.
What's that you say?
Can you really think it's yours!

Spring's Decree

I'm worried about the willow.
For weeks now it's been spraying
the still ripe lawn with its pale dead leaves
while the surrounding amber trees,
lit by a low sun, cling tightly to theirs.
Usually it's the last to go.

From where I stand its once domed, regal
branches seem like broken twigs, skeletal,
doing as the wind bids. Will it come
back next year? Will the fact that
someone cares help it endure?

It's been a year of human loss, too,
and while love and care assuaged,
in the end they couldn't cure.
Am I reading something into this?

Soon, inevitably, winter will have its
unpredictable way. Will that sick tree
survive, regain its potency? We can only
wait for the seasons to turn, and for
omnipotent spring to issue its decree.

Full Moon in Normandy

Excitedly, you call me to the window.
It's 2am, and a spectacular moon is aiming an
eerie spotlight at the outstretched trees below.
The scene is set for an all-star show.

As sporadic gusts of wind grab them by the throat,
ghost-like bushes, bathed in white, dance a war dance
on the lawn. Our tiny pond has become a moat.
Although summer, the grass is wearing its winter coat.

To us it seemed a magical moment, heaven sent,
its spell still infiltrating the darkened room and bed
where, huddled together, we finally lay, quite spent,
our spinning minds continuing to fantasize and invent.

Vigil

I don't accuse,
am on my guard,
that's all.

I won't forget they tried
to wipe my broken
people
from the earth – no,
not them, of course, too
young, their fathers or their
fathers' fathers – not even
them, perhaps.
Be fair.

They might, who knows,
have been among those
righteous brave who
in reaching out their hands
sealed their own fate,
or simply those who turned
away, afraid. Perhaps.
Impossible to conceive
the fear, the shadows of
the night, the bootsteps
on the stair.

Now, a life-time later,
alone beneath the Bahnhoff's
amber lights, incessant
rain machine-gunning the
roof's grim glass, I tell
myself the hordes
I watch there, fighting
their way towards the waiting
trains – *achtung* – late for
work or hurrying home,
that they could not

themselves have heard
the shots, the muzzled
cries, the dogs, the
clank, clank, clank
of the nightmare trucks
departing on cue for their
one-way journey to Hell
(from which of these platforms
I wonder – one, two?)

and that looking back
aghast, perhaps, at those black
Wagnerian scenes, history
to them, however obscene,
that they, contrite perhaps,
would wash their hands
in innocence at night –
not, like some demented Lady
Macbeth, scrub scrub
scrubbing
to expunge the dead, as
those accursed others should.
Sins of the fathers
heavy on their head.
Be fair.

And yet, and yet...
It's seventy years since
that war began, but if
I, a Jew, scion
of that haunted race,
forget, who will remember,
and if none remembers, the
dead are truly dead.

I don't accuse,
am on my guard,
that's all.

Baker Street Return

'Aren't you...?'
he suddenly whispered
looking over his laptop
throwing out my name
...and I had to admit
I was, the very same.

He'd been eyeing me
since Baker Street in a
way he thought discreet.
Someone from my past
it seemed, but who?
As the personal nature of
his questions grew I tried
to find some kind of clue.

But then the name tab
on his case caught my
eye and the jigsaw pieces
of a school boy's face
fell slowly into place.

That was him, of course, that
old class photo, dark-haired
sitting to my right – a nippy
inside-left as I recall. Hard
to equate this well-dressed
grey-haired man with those
bellicose boys who raised
such hell. I'm sure he thought
the same of me as well.

'I never go back', he confided,
'hated the place, means nothing now.
They're all dead anyhow.
And you?'

And me?
'Not yet' I wanted to quip, but
'me too' I wryly said instead.
My stop at last. I wished him well
and waved a warm goodbye.
In a strange kind of way
he'd made my day.

But it's not quite true I told
myself thinking back as I
mounted the moving stairs
and voices, faces, images
I hadn't heard or seen for years
gate-crashed my head.

Disturbed, it seems the dead
weren't quite that dead.

In Good Stead

I wasn't much of a pupil, I must admit,
and he, stooped gentle man, was no great sage.
Yet somehow we stumbled through the Hebrew
alphabet – *aleph, bet... gimel... daled, hey*,
studied fading texts, and come the day
and 13 struck, I knew my party piece OK.

It was to hold me in good stead, and when
in time love wove it's magic thread and under
the chuppah, in wonder, we sacredly wed,
again the ancient words broke through:
With this ring, *betabaat zu*.

The glass smashed (*Mazal Tov!*) and you –
thank the good Lord – mine, how that old
teacher would have enjoyed the wine!

Now, on Festivals and Friday nights,
when evenings dim and the mesmeric
light of candles reigns, the familiar
melodies, letters, words converge again,
reclaim memories half-shed, a boy's
urgent words in an ageing man's head.

And when, dreadfully, dear ones disappear,
and I'm called upon once more to recite
that mournful liturgy, sad leaves shrouding
the waiting grave, no mention of death
in the prayer for the dead, those letters, words
are there again, though faltering on the tongue,
meaning temporarily astray, while
the silent language of tears holds sway.

No, I was no great pupil, but that kind old man –
now gone, no doubt, to the great *cheder* in the sky –
knew what he was about, never a sharp word,
never a shout. Searching the alphabet I try,
as those early years, unbidden, disturbingly stir,
to find the words to repay my debt, come
back to just these potent two: a*leph*, *bet*.

Wallflowers

Those defiant poppies
on the bank are back, amidst
the show-off blossom from
the cherry tree and the daffodils'
dainty pas de deux.

'Look at us' they seem to say
in their arresting way, 'we're here for
all to see, ignore our regal finery
and we might as well not be'.

It used to be like that at those
Saturday evening dances, the
focus of our teenage week: the
over-coiffed girls along the walls,
all fancy-dressed and 'look at me',
waiting to be asked; and we,
young boys on the town (or so
we thought), all brylcreemed and
silk-tied, standing back, dreading
a rebuff. Until someone dared,
and then we'd all rush in.

That last dance was the important thing,
moving closer inch by inch for the kill,
the thrill of a possible kiss or clinch
as you walked her slowly home, stood
uncertainly outside her parents' door.
But nothing more.
Such wasted opportunities!

Meanwhile, back on the hill, the sun
drops behind the darkening trees
and the poppies are taking their evening
curtain call, oblivious of the embarrassing
memories they had sparked, not waiting
to be asked, and triumphant to the last.

Time on My Hands

I've got time on my hands
this summer night, and the stars
are at their most spectacular.

I should write Odes to the Gods
as the foam-mouthed waves crash
onto the empty sands below, but
thoughts of you fill my head instead.

I'd wish you here, now, to share
the wonder of it all, but they won't
care a jot if you are or not.

And when the stars are usurped,
a bragging sun holds sway, and those
waves pound on dispassionately

all that time I foolishly thought
mine will have been through
my hands, and away.

Last Stand

All that's left now is an old bay
window centring a high brick wall,
lonely as a widow. Nothing supports it.
It looks as if a sudden gust of wind
would send it crashing.

Below, rubble all around, a grey
rainbow of dust choking the air.
Ashes to ashes.

It's very like those pictures
of the war, except there are
warning signs everywhere you
can hardly ignore: Danger. Keep
Out. Demolition in Progress.

No such warnings then.
Now men in white helmets
soldier the place. No sirens,
no air raids, no white lights
igniting a threatening sky.

Soon it will be rebuilt, ad hoc,
to meet a developer's design.
Flats perhaps, an old people's
home, a bland office block.

Yet for all that, something seems
wrong, a grand old house nearly
gone, with all its secret history.

What love has been made behind
that darkened window, I wonder,
and what deaths, perhaps, have
brought their own devastation?

Drawn in, I watch a crane, high
as the sky, lift a massive concrete
block from here to there. No alarms.

On the face of it everything is calm,
but that wall, with its solitary window,
looks ever more vulnerable.

Still, for the moment, like a
theatre tableau, it stands proudly
there, deserving applause,
though we know its time will
come, and the curtains close.

Just in Case

That wonder conker always took the prize.
It wasn't just its size. Wrapped and stored
through winter, soaked in vinegar, I pulled
all the tricks it took to win, and time and
again bragging rivals would be left staring
foolishly at a dangling piece of string.

And whenever autumn winds attacked and
fresh conkers fell like stones from the giant
trees near the old school gate, and though it
was strictly out of bounds, we'd be racing
there like hounds once the break bell went.
The spoils were rich but the risks great, and
we kept a wary watch for any mean masters
who might be lying in wait... just in case.

A lifetime later, strolling alone along a gusty
country lane, the memory tapes spun suddenly
back as I spotted dozens of newly-fallen ones
lying invitingly at my feet, their abandoned shells
scattered open-mouthed among
the rain-soaked, yellowing leaves.

What varnished beauties they were,
what champions they would have made!
The schoolboy I once was would have
grabbed the lot, subjected them to his
deceitful wizardry, and I couldn't
pass them by now just like that.

Scanning them with expert eyes
I pocketed the biggest for old time's
sake, bagging a few more tempting ones
for luck. Then, looking furtively round, and as
a ghostly dusk began to settle on the place,
I beat a guilty retreat... just in case.

Handle with Care

What a colourful Monday
morning that was. Not because
war was declared or some
dictator toppled, not because
England finally got the Aussies
in a spin, or scored a startling
World Cup shoot-out win.

But simply because there,
on the floor, to the right
of the door, on the 8.20 am
number 13 bus, at the foot
of the stairs, a pair of scarlet
knickers provocatively lay –
just what was needed to
kick-start the day.

Quite how they got there
and, most intriguingly, whose
they were – questions that
hung tantalisingly in the air.
This, after all, was a respectable
route, not backstreet Pigalle, not
the Folies Bergère, where a flash
of this or that was de rigueur.

Why take them down here?
With so much to behold, how bold.
Imagination starts to unfold.
Was she slim, was she tall, blonde,
brunette, a grande horizontale, a
femme fatale? When the wind
blows, won't she be cold?

Doubtless the worldly French
would have shrugged it off,
winking at one another,
knowingly. Some frustrated
Madame Bovary on the loose,
perhaps – and in sober, religious
Golders Green what's more.
Encore!

But no cheers from us, not on
that bus. Nobody exchanged
a glance, all looked the other way
askance, tiptoed daintily round,
exited swiftly into the welcome
street without a sound.

What, I wondered, will London
Transport do? Wear rubber gloves,
blow them up, handle with care?
Put them in a plain brown wrapper,
Return to Sender (wherever she be
after her late night bender)?
Place an ad in the local rag?
Lost, one pair of scarlet knickers,
owner sought. Apply in person,
bring proof where bought.

Anyway, no time to think of that,
must get on, there's a train to catch
a serious day to hatch, and
besides, if she's going to apply
I'd best make sure I'm back and
waiting there... or will my scarlet
lady spoil the fun, not care,
go out and buy herself another pair?

Taking Stock

Those musty albums must have lain for years
under the stairs. And what a rum lot of characters
they reveal, posing for eternity. But my,
how they keep their guards up high.

Those starch-collared ancients, were they
ever young I wonder? And those stately ladies
at their sides, with their floor long touch-me-not skirts,
a hidden armoury of armour beneath – were they?
Who can tell. We know them only as Great
Uncle this or Great Aunt that, stern,
forbidding, formal as hell.

Yet think of all the children they begot –
seven, ten, a dozen, even more.
They weren't brought by the stork I'll bet.
And consider their names... Max, Amelia,
Manny, Rose, Morris (known as Morrie)
Girtie the Flirty, lovely Harriet.

Go back a little, imagine them human, imagine
them young, in love, cutting a dash, hot,
finding a niche when niches were hard to find
in starch-stiff Victorian England – especially since,
it must be said, mostly they were a foreign lot.

By and large, though, save for a few bad'uns
I could name, their dreams came right just
the same and they could proudly pose for those
puff-chested photographs in black and white.

What though, I wonder, would they say,
seeing us now, long-haired, be-jeaned, dusting
them down, we, the future they made love for,
built for, prayed for – but proud of them all,
come what may, and with them all the way.

Blues in the Park

The landscape changes by the day,
haunting our lives in many furtive ways.

It's not just the failing sun, the ghosts
of darkening evenings creeping in
that halts the step, not the steady drip
of leaves from widowed trees, great
oaks felled, the rows of shattered
flowers gunned down by feckless winds

it's not just that: a season gone, a
season lost with all its rainbow colours,
autumn's melancholy catalogue.

It's the human landscape, altering by
the hour, by the minute, that makes
one falter – the shrinking list of friends
you'd meant to call but never quite
got round to, the tables you can no
longer fill, the dwindling cast at
family celebrations, grave occasions,
houses boarded up, their owners gone
moved permanently on, letters
Returned to Sender. The litany of loss.
Grief always just a phone call away.

Walking tonight, arm in arm in
the park we love just before closing
time, shadows are everywhere.
Passing the animal enclosures,
the children's roundabout and swings,
the spread-eagled oak, we finally reach
the old Victorian bandstand from which,
one glorious summer Sunday, to
our delight, exultant jazz exploded.
'The Humphrey Lyttelton Band', a board
announced, and so it was. Applause.

A care-free crowd lined the surrounding
lawn, danced and jived as we so often
had to that same anarchic virtuoso, birds
taking fright as his trumpet soared.

Now, as we skirt the lawn's damp edge,
silence rules. The desolate bandstand
seems bereft, no trumpet beckons,
no 'Bad Penny Blues', no 'Careless Love'.
Birds eerily line the wooden rails, waiting
for God knows who. Rain and darkness brew.

The landscape changes by the second.

Jazz at St Pancras

for Anthony Harkavy

'Play me' invited the piano on
the booming station concourse
and play it with brio the pianist
did, dodging the duff notes:
'Georgia on my Mind' as I recall,
which wasn't on many people's
that wet Monday morning.

Gradually, improbably,
St Pancras Station had started
to swing, with one couple clinched
in a dance and others gathering
round appreciatively.
A woman with a wobbly
voice began to sing.

Then slowly, as the rhythm
rose and the jazz flowed, six
tall young boys with grey college
scarves edged towards the
piano from the back, laying
careful hands on it in turn
as if the wood they were
touching was holy wood.

When, smiling, they turned away,
the large white hearing aids they
wore came startlingly into view,
and the amazed throng parted
for them like the biblical sea
of old, having witnessed the
surreal scene and understood.

Clearly, those boys had heard a melody
we could not, and suddenly the
station was no longer cold, and there
was more than music in the air.

Keeping Up with the T★★★★

From the asterisks in today's *Times*
it's not, it seems, the Ps and Qs
you have to mind, but the Fs and Cs.
What delicate times are these!

Strange, the four-letter and other
words you can, and those you can't.
If you're hankering after the word
that rhymes with front, you'll
clearly have to find another slant

and if it's the one that chimes with
buck, there's no way round, you'll
have to duck. Bollocks too are
clearly out, but tits, by all accounts,
are firmly in. What sin!

You can shag these days to your
heart's content, and score and lay,
and even the occasional orgasm's OK
(though talk of come's not done).
And love's still good, if a bit passé.

You can be a bore and talk of war,
of porn and rape, but also, I read
today, fellate. Crumpet (though
best not trumpet it) is permitted too,
so long as it's good for you.

As for WAGs, what they do and
what they don't, what they will
and what they won't, is all the rage,
splashed brazenly across the page.

But when you come to those
salacious two, prick and screw,
take care, as asterisks will doubtless
flare – unless, of course, its needlework
or carpentry you're referring to.

You just never know what
a carless word might do.

Master Strokes

I

To hell with domesticity!
Unlike the sober couples
in those Dutch interiors
Chagall's rainbow lovers
have the freedom of the
Moscow skies to fly and
frolic in, obliviously.

II

Thanks, Pablo...
So *that's* where it is!
All those anatomy
lessons could have
been given a miss.
Clearly though it's
a contortionist you'd
need to be to satisfy
her satisfactorily!

III

Leonardo's ladies
are hard to resist:
the one with the
enigmatic smile
and Italian name
who draws them by
the coachload to her
quarters by the Seine,
and his ethereal Virgin
of those mysterious
rocks, that infant
at her feet. A miracle
that's hard to beat.

IV

That defiant sunflower
battling the wind has
Van Gogh's name all over it.
While his landscapes
with their fiery colour
remain startling testaments
to his power, his troubled
psyche cost him dear,
a word that fittingly
rhymes with ear.

V

Señor Dali, ever the
grandmaster of deceit.
I'm never sure
whether that's a clock
or a door, that a lump
of meat or a cat on heat.
And isn't that your cock
in the corner there?
Anything to make them stare.

Sins on the Water

Cast onto the water like that
will those sins sink or float, I
wonder, as I watch that ancient
ritual from a distant river bank?
And how will all those unsuspecting
creatures of the deep react
to such seemingly lethal bait
invading their private habitat?

Will they swallow them whole
(will the good Lord, Blessed be He?),
or will they simply nudge them aside
(will He?) as they glide through the
reeds that hug the river bed?
Mysterious indeed are the ways
of the On High, and of the deep.

Now, as another year turns, we too,
less observant but no less true,
must respond in our own way to the
continuing draw of the Days of Awe,
atone, begin anew, or endeavour to
as the Sages urge, though some we
love will have fallen by the way,
and there are wars and scars we
know the prayers of holy men won't
erase, even as we say, in whatever
tongue, All Praise.

Note
On the Jewish New Year, the start of the Ten Days of Awe which culminate
in The Day of Atonement, many orthodox Jews observe the ritual of
symbolically casting their sins onto the water of a nearby river or lake.

Last Lines

for Vernon Scannell

I've been reading again the
powerful poem you sent me
just before you died. You
called it your last, though
there were several brave and
poignant others with it in
that unexpected envelope,
and a scribbled note that ended
'no need to respond, love V'.

How typical that they should be
about your craft at such a time,
and the books surrounding you
queuing to be read, but evoke
also memories of Fitzrovia bars and
Paris dives, and love that landed
telling blows too often low.

Oh yes there were the boxing
references there as well, for though
a shy and courteous man you'd
had your moments in the ring
and always took your chance to
work its language in, along with
haunting images that reek of war,
the cursed theme that never let you
go and you could never shirk, shadowing
your life and most enduring work.

You lived it all, and it's all here,
final lines that raise a moving cheer.
We'll drink a hearty round to them,
or two, or three, and to you, your
work, your memory, as you would
surely have encouraged us to do.
How mean you can't drink too!

Taking Me Back

for Carole

That was a magical walk you took me on.
What did I expect? Crocodiles leaping from the Nile?
The enigmatic Sphinx resolving its own riddles?
Cleopatra plying her seductive trade in the market square?

No, there were wonders enough in more earthly
things. Your hieroglyphic smile as we strolled that
memorable mile was every bit their exotic match.
So too the conferring elders, clasping
their hookah pipes in the packed cafés,

the rattling carts and kerb-side stalls,
the date palms and sycamores acknowledging
the breeze, pointing the way, the
intoxicating blend of spices in the air –
coriander, cumin, caraway, myrrh –
hot pitta bread, the scent of sand.
Everywhere the plaintive call to prayer.

The band of jean-clad youths who followed in
our wake, touting their wares, tugging at our sleeves, could
not have known this was, for you, a kind of pilgrimage,
childhood landmarks alive at every stage.

How often, in safe hospitable London, you talked
of this, awake or in sleep, and now here it all was,
a touch away, no longer myth. There, real as day,
masked by fig and olive trees, set back, your

family flat, giant geraniums trailing from the
balcony's rail. Next door, the makeshift
laundry-cum-store you would vividly recall,
steam still hissing from behind its wall.

Further on, the midday sun intense, your school,
and there, beyond the barriers, the famed
Gezira Sporting Club, less vibrant now than then,
where your sports-mad father Ben hit a vaunted
century against an English team – match won –
that was to stand him in good stead.

Here, on the expansive terrace, the oblivious ladies
sought the shade, drank tea, played bridge.
Circling it all, a racecourse where no horses run.
Excitedly, you find the pool where you learnt to swim.
So many memories to be taken in.

Later, after a siesta, following the tourist route to
the Pyramids, near the elegant Mena House
where you had your birthday teas, you laughed
to catch your English husband getting
the hump from a camel, falling to his knees.
Something you never thought to see!

Then, don't blink, across the mystic Nile,
relief from the heat, the historic ice-cream
parlour, Groppi, your childhood treat.
Turning back for more you caught your foot
on the uneven floor, stumbled into the street:
so many tantalizing flavours, hard to ignore.

Nearby, still there, its once regal facade
sulking in the shade, the cinema where, aged
twelve, entranced, you wept your way through your
first grown-up film, *Gone with the Wind* – and watched
your last, before being forced, in '56, to flee.
Gone, indeed. War's continuing history.

Night's all-encompassing mirage.
Despite the desecration – the pillaged gravestones
of Saqquara, the mummies staring into space
in the museum's large air-conditioned halls –
the darkness brings the centuries
back, restores their dignity.

Jackals howling, snakes uncoiling, with night
the desert too reclaims its awesome majesty,
stars splattering the vast Arabian sky,
while scorpions prepare their lethal sting,
eagles stir, and the mighty Pharaohs,
their curses heard at last, finally sleep.

A Small Reward

Those few small coins tossed into
the old guitar case at the busker's feet
are a small reward for the pleasure
unexpected music brings.

It might be a Dylan or a Beatles tune
that hits you as you ride the escalator down
making you want to sing, or perhaps a snatch
of Mozart, or a harp's melodious theme.

Today, in the rush hour, it was 'Where Have
All the Flowers Gone', fervently sung,
yesterday an accordionist playing 'La Vie en Rose',
touching off Left-Bank memories.

Mostly people stride swiftly by, averting
their eyes, embarrassed it would seem, but
often I find myself irresistibly drawn in.

Not all the performers are talented, or young,
and the screeches of wobbly flutes and shaky
violins also fill the stations' echoing corridors.
But some quite clearly are.

What, I wonder, could their true ambitions be.
Will that stirring tenor voice or finely modulated
cantata, that guitarist's flamenco lament or
jazzman's driving beat, eventually bring cheering
audiences to their feet with calls for more?

For the moment, though, they are ours, here
underground, shifting a mood, lightening the day,
and worth every carefully thrown penny, I'd say.

The Old Couple

On the dance floor, in bed, they know each other's moves,
it's all been carefully choreographed over long years.

And even if the mood is black, if something irritates
and an old unsettled score erupts, the cautious
words they use will have all been used before.
Nothing detracts or detonates.

Shadows of former hurts may lie in wait,
round corridors, across the floor, but somehow
they glide round them with no apparent show
he this way, her that, quick quick slow.

It's another kind of dance that has kept them
together all this time. And though the tune
may have vanished somewhere in the air,
the harmony they share is touchingly still there
complete, and beyond any conductor's beat.

No Change

Fashions change,
but never yours.
With a beard
and hat
like that
they'd spot you any day.
You'd never get away.

Vilna
Vitebsk
Stamford Hill
Golders Green.
Same old scene.

Times were
you'd have been
stoned on sight,
or rounded up
as you went to pray.
With those
sidelocks,
also, perhaps,
the stocks.

But not here, today.
I'd like to think so
anyway. For not
to be free is a
kind of blasphemy.

And though, like
those other cults and
creeds attired in
yellow, pink, red,
or burka-black

who grace our streets,
you often turn my head
even inspire a little dread
(I know you shouldn't
and wish you wouldn't)

clearly yours is a uniform
that's seen horrific days.
So who are we, in our
jean-clad, mini-skirted,
impious world, to wish
it, or you, away.

A Doctor's Call

for Joe

They seemed so magical at the time,
those giant round bottles with their
technicolor liquids igniting the glass –
red, purple, blue, dazzling green –
all plastered with fading white labels
and scrawled Latin words whose
meanings I could never glean.

Alluringly displayed in the dispensary
my father had alongside his surgery,
they were as mysterious to me as
a witch's brew, and even more
intriguing than the jars of humbugs,
gobstoppers, liquorice and more
that lay in wait at the corner store.

They were his own special mix
and I'd watch enthralled as he shook,
stirred, measured and poured the
strange-smelling concoctions, while
his patients waited trustingly behind
the adjacent surgery door. Amazingly
most came back for more!

A doctor of the old school, he was
part of their lives, knew them better
than they knew themselves, and they
loved him for it: half the cure, I'm sure.

And there was humour too. I fondly
recall the corny cartoons on the wall
behind his desk – a woman told to undress
replying, 'you first, doctor, I'm shy',
and a man, pointing to a urine bottle
high on a shelf, 'what, from here?'.

Surgery over, he'd be off on his rounds –
in an old black Vauxhall, as I recall –
then back home for the evening shift.
More medicine poured, more pulses calmed.

When, seventy striking, he felt it time
to hang up his stethoscope, his bereft
patients hurried round, children in tow,
to shake his hand, many leaving small gifts –
wine, chocolates, home-made cake.
It seemed to him a kind of wake!

Then, fragile years later, on one indelible
day, his own faltering heart finally gave way.
Dismayed, I found myself surveying the drips
and tubes and the frightening battery of
machines they tried to save him with, and
thought back to those bottled cures of his.

Who knows, they may just have done the trick.

Still Life

A family's colourful history in photos old
and new stretches along the flaking walls
of the flat's long corridor – fading
formal portraits, bouquet-clasping
brides forever draped in white, children
knee-deep in sand, the waves rolling in,
babies, parties, festive occasions.
Smile for the camera.

But for all that, it's your tatty old hats
and faded woollen scarves still hanging
by the door, askew, that always hold
my eye – and that old stick of yours,
still showing signs of mud, as if you were
just back from an outing to the park.

Time to give them away, I hear
the chorus say, but no, I can't
let them go, for as long as they
are there, then you, for me, are
too, and every bit as real as all
those photos on the wall, and the
vivid scenes they movingly recall.

Who Was Who

Such deeds! Surely, no mere mortals could have
performed all these. Those daily obits of the famous
dead, whether of rogue or sage, read like fiction now.

How ignorant, how inadequate, they make one feel,
how captivating they unfailingly are, and the photos –
often black-and-white or sepia – add their own
poignancy; but the person's dead whatever's said.
No jobs to be got from those CVs!

Who's Who won't list them anymore, their
clubs will pay them homage with much grace,
then fill their place. They are no more real
now really than those many unsung others

who slipped more privately away on the
same black day: no medals to display
no great public deeds to salute, no works of
literature or art, peaks climbed, matches won,
life-saving discoveries, stirring symphonies.

Were they all really here? Indeed they were,
though writing of them turns them into history.
Just ask those dear ones left behind, bereft,
living in shadows, fighting back tears, photos
on the windowsill cataloguing the years.

Real, all right, they'd say, their impassioned
memories fuelled by love or guilt or even rage
and different in every way from those other
measured words we read and marvel at each day,
anonymous and distant on a transient page.

Some of Those Days

for my mother, Charlotte

There were days when fingers
stormed those fading keyboards,
but now, lonely by the fireplace,
that old Grand piano has no voice.

Somehow, though, it still retains its mahogany
dignity, covered as it is these days by a
canopy of family photos in silver frames
and the occasional flash of freshly cut flowers.

Frail now, but just as dignified, you sang then with
such pizazz, while my father, ever your accompanist,
raced behind you on those keys, all rhythm and bounce.

At the sudden memory of the impromptu
songs my parents would launch into,
and that sweet voice, my toes begin to tap –
'Some of These Days', your party piece,
as poignant and transporting as ever.

By chance, at an Old Time Variety show friends took
us to the other night, an artiste sang that song
amidst blue Max Miller jokes you'd have died for,
loving that saucy showman as you do.

Yet yours was the voice I heard, not hers,
and that old piano's too, striding behind, revived.
For my money, you topped the bill that night
and always will…
but oh, how we'll miss you honey.

From Time to Time

Some roots are easily dislodged –
a sharp twist of fork or trowel
and unwanted weeds go flying.
A number, more stubborn, demand a
larger fork or spade, fight a tougher fight
but in the end give way. A few
hang tightly in and win the day.

Part of nature's game, our own roots
are much the same, seem to be
shrugged off easily enough
until an accent slips, a slight hits
sharply home, a hand is raised,
a look in a glass betrays.

Even now, surprised, from
time to time I hear the Northern
vowels my father never really shed
and the even stronger accents
of his own parents – his pious Russian
father with his stern rabbinical beard,
his Polish-German mother forever
rattling off Chopin Polonaises on the
old upright as if nothing had changed.

Transported, I recall their rambling
house in Leeds where my father spent
his early years, the grandfather clock
at the foot of the creaking stairs,
and above all the deep coal house
by the black back door I always kept well
clear of, believing ghosts hid there.

I cherish them, those revolving scenes
I sometimes visit in my dreams,
and those vibrant voices, for though
distant, they're my voices too,
affecting all I say, and do.

The Party's Over

The fizz has gone, and those
abandoned bottles, coffined in black
plastic boxes in the street, give no hint
of the jollity they doubtless brought.
Like fish betrayed by the tide, stranded
on the beach, they seem to be staring
open-mouthed into a morning-after sky
way beyond their reach.

What the celebration was I'll never know –
a landmark birthday or anniversary perhaps,
or more excitingly, a lover's tryst?
Not my affair anyway, a stranger
in the November mist.

As if on cue, an old Cole Porter song
invades my head – 'French champagne,
so good for the brain'. Sinatra and Bing.
Imagine how many have gone down
to their seductive swing!

The band plays on.
Whether French or not, whatever
the brand, I tell myself, whistling along,
it always seems to score – skirts,
gowns, crinkled shirts and more
strewn along the floor.

As the music fades, the trees that line
the street, almost leafless now, seem
to embrace my meditative mood,
and the willow too at the lawn's edge,
contorted by the wind into a ghost-like face.

It's that time of year, and we wait
in limbo for the months to spring
their startling change, for the band
to re-assemble in the wings, for
bottles to be cooled, glasses charged.

'Another bride, another groom...'

Same old tunes, same old game.
We prepare ourselves to play it again.

White Surprise

Not being the Alps, nor even near,
there was not supposed to be snow
in our steep-sloping street, especially
as winter had begun its retreat.

So when, stealthily in the night,
it smothered everything in sight,
the Sunday morning scene
that hit our sleep-filled eyes
caught us by surprise.

Instead of cars, excited children
on toboggans and make-shift trays
swept daringly down the white-clad
road without a care, screams
and wild laughter in the air.

A giant snowman, with marzipan lips
and someone's old pipe in its mouth,
also appeared to be having a laugh.
Another, with twigs for pigtails, sported
a bright red cap and an Arsenal scarf.

When, later in the day, we emerged
to join the fray, 'what fun' you said,
even as a snowball grazed your head.

Then, surreally, like something
out of a Lowry picture or a dream,
a lame fox limped painfully past
through the snow, ignoring us all,
its brown coat dangerously on show,
its zigzagging footsteps aglow.

And though everything is now
as if it had never been, it was
all vividly there that day, and
in my mind is here to stay.

Taken Aback

I knew these streets
like the back of my hand,
those shops, that well-kept
park, the wooden bridge,
the murky stream beneath.
This is where I sowed my
teenage oats on dark
Saturday nights when
winter shuffled in, suffered
embarrassing defeats, came
back again for more like
some punch-drunk pug
who won't hang up his gloves,
believes he still can win.
Illusions constant tug.

Here I roamed on foot
where now I drive, ran for
the last bus home, wiped
lipstick from my lips when
luck was in, made light of
it when it was clearly not.
It always seemed like love,
but who can say?
How innocent those days,
the fumblings behind that
broken fence, the constant fray.

Long gone the dance hall
where we rocked around the
clock, shimmied, waltzed
and jived below the spinning
lights. Gone too the Odeon
on the corner where on
wet Sunday afternoons
we'd bag the back row seats,
planting a casual hand
on hers, stealing a kiss.
Now blocks of faceless
flats and late night
stores regale the streets.

I did not count on this,
following this route by
chance after all these years.
Pulling sharply up at the
kerb to take things in,
memories hurtle by, disturb.
I stare at distant doors
I once went through,
vainly search my mind
for faces, names.
Where have they gone,
where indeed have I ?

I'm forced, it seems,
as insistent ghosts descend,
to meet it all anew,
pretend it's as it was,
be led astray – until, that is,
the red lights switch again
to beckoning green and
impatient hooters intervene,
break the fading spell,
propel me on my way,
make it aggressively clear
the make-believe is dead,
that there's an all-demanding
present to confront instead.

At Ease

At ease and approaching
the bus stop where I stood,
the fair-haired soldier, on leave,
perhaps, or returning from it,
saluted suddenly, passing
the poppied memorial on
his right, not losing a step.

A dutiful gesture? Respect for
those poor sods who'd lost the fight?
It seemed more telling than a
formal military parade, bugle call,
or a however-many-guns salute,
and in its simple way, as memorable.

Close of Play

Out! The umpire's imperious finger
brooks no argument – leg before,
bungling a drive through the covers,
missing the bowler's spin.
I'd have much preferred leg-over.

The number of times I'd been
told, keep your head down,
eye on the ball, follow through...
but with so many mini-skirted wonders
on the boundary that day my eyes
were understandably elsewhere.

I'd planned to hit sixes and fours
all round the wicket, be the
centre of their applause and talk.
Instead I had to walk.

It only takes the sensuous smell
of just-cut grass to draw me back
to that school-boy afternoon, making
me endure once more the bowler's
jubilant cheer, the trek back to the
pavilion, the stark figure nought
jeering from a timeless board.

Those half-smiles and sympathetic
looks from the players' sisters and
their even more desirable mothers
in their clinging summer frocks
was not what I'd oiled my bat for.

Cheers should have been ringing
in my ears, nods and suggestive winks
the order of the day, covers of
a different kind teasing my mind.

Over the years there would be
many games like that, embarrassingly
recalled, so many times run out,
caught, bowled middle stump.
Occasionally, of course, I've had
triumphant times, won the day
(of course I have, I must have done)
but I'd be hard put to name just one.

Always it's the red-faced moments
that continue to haunt and flare,
any so-called successes difficult
to prove or maintain, impossible
to ensnare, never quite there.

That's the human game we play,
over after over, until the last ball
has been bowled, another umpire
calls a halt for fading light, and the
fragile bails are finally removed.

Hospital Notes

Tripoli's ablaze, and as chanting
rebels raze his Presidential compound
Gaddafi, like a rat, has gone to ground.
But here, within these four London walls,
another battle's being waged.

'I can't remember your name'.
When a mother says that to her son
it seems the end of the game.
We must continue just the same.

There's fire in her eyes as we ease
some food between reluctant lips.
She won't take what she doesn't like,
but then she never would! That's good.
We give her drinks she hardly sips.

When I crack a feeble joke to stay
her straying mind, she manages a grin.
'Cheeky thing', she says, and winks.
What is it that she thinks?

This, we are told, is a fight she cannot win,
she's old, her life's been rich.
We've heard those lines before,
it's a script we'd like to ditch.

She's been with us for all our years
and it's our turn now. We'll man
the barricades as best we can.

As always, my father's photo watches
from her bedside table. A doctor, he'd
be relieved to see her stable.

A kind nurse adds a little brandy to her drink.
She beams a smile again.
'*Le chayim*', we hear her quietly proclaim.
She calls me by my name.

A toast to life.
The mood's completely changed.
There's talk now of her going home.
She's sitting upright in a chair,
no longer seems deranged.

She looks towards the door. Born in
1914, she knows a thing or two about war
and will defy them all once more.

I raise an imaginary machine gun to
the sky to let triumphant bullets fly.

23 August 2011

Year after Year

I watched an ageing monarch
lay a wreath to the Glorious Dead.
'It's a long Way to Tipperary', those troops
had sung, and 'We'll Meet Again',
but meet they never would.

Cruelly released from the hell
in which they found themselves,
with many ending up beneath the
earth on which they fell, it's hard
to see the glory in their story.
Yet year after year she's there.

Later that week, passing
by chance the Cenotaph I'd seen
on TV, lined with dignitaries, my eyes
were drawn unexpectedly to row
upon row of rain-soaked wreaths.

Each one overlapping the next,
in the eerie light of a November
evening they seemed like corpses,
the blood-red of their poppies staining
the white stone. Ghosts everywhere.

And though the wind and rain were
playing havoc with the names and notes
attached, some remained stirringly clear –
from The Free French, famous regiments,
different cities, faiths – poignant words from
those who knew their worth, and held them dear.

Collage

Seven fifty-three, and as the bus heaves
forward jerkily, a collage of disparate
scenes distracts my still cloudy eyes:

the curve of grey rails on a white balcony
the redness of the bricks below, the way they overlap,

a fence over there that's lost its slats,
a grimy car in need of a clean, a
front door's sickly shade of green.

So many Shops to Let, Sales Agreed.

A dramatically tall woman in villainous
black stands at a bus stop, scarlet lips
igniting her powder-white face,

a dog has a man on the end of a lead,
two cats eye each other gingerly,
a snail has patterned the still wet street.

At the side of a run-down house, a
builder, cigarette in hand, leans beneath
his ladder brazenly, an empty bench
waits at the turn of the road.

There used to be a conductor calling
'fares please', but now a solitary driver
watches as the passengers coil in,
touch home their cards religiously.

Three stops to go.
My book, unopened on my knee,
stares back at me.

No angels hover, no star from the East,
my mind in free-fall now, released.

A Great Pianist Hangs up His Hands

for Alfred Brendel

That you'd decided to call it a day was bad enough,
the audience on their feet calling for yet another
encore as you took your final bow. No one wished
to believe your Odyssey complete
...or let you leave.

But today, in the silence of your London home,
you confess you no longer play now even for yourself.
Your hearing, down a notch or two, distorts the piano's
sound, the notes no longer true, intolerable.
You relate this over tea, philosophically.

For us, fortunately, the spell of your discs persists,
so we hear you playing even when you aren't.
For you, life's focus shifts.

You give master classes, work with
string quartets – the sound of the strings
still mercifully true – write, lecture,
give readings of your poems, distil
your thoughts... and afterthoughts.

All this you convey in your precise, fervent way,
and all the while your right hand seems to be
tapping out sonatas, non-stop, on you knee.
Beethoven would have seen the irony.

Sickert's Lady

All the way from seedy Camden Town
and there, in a smart Belgravia home,
you are, hanging provocatively above
the well-stocked bar. A bottle of gin
(Tanqueray, the very best) points
pointedly at your right breast.

His brush raised high, his glass
double-charged, how that womanizing
painter you loved to model for would
have laughed, seeing you there in
that gold-edged frame, your worldly
eyes tamed at last, and that knowing
smile that would have made the
Mona Lisa run a mile...

and not a drink to be had, for all your guile.

The Anonymous Man

I am the anonymous man.
I walk in shadows, furtively,
enter rooms when no-one's there,
dodge the stranger on the stair.

I seek the cover of the night
hide my identity, keep out of sight.
Darkened windows draw my gaze,
and lamplights ghostly in the haze.

My complexion's pale, my
suit a neutral shade of grey.
My demeanour, mean, gives little away.
I fear the brilliance of the day.

If challenged, I'll smile blankly back,
adopt all kinds of cunning subterfuge
to confuse my inquisitor, get off the rack.

The eye I turn is invariably blind.
Ignoring this, evading that,
I seem to wear a stranger's hat.

I've spent a lifetime hiding all I can
I've yet to find out who I am.

Gone

Looking in the mirror
I see your eyes and hair.
The more I stand there looking,
The more I see your stare.

A summer's gone, a winter's been,
You left without a word.
Whenever there are voices,
I think it's yours I've heard.

Then when rain disperses
And suddenly there's sun,
I feel the warmth descending,
Think you must have come.

And now that winter's struck again
While frost and snow abound,
I see you still at every turn,
Yet know you won't be found.

Almost Fatal

Not such a fantasy
sometimes, that almost
fatal urge, coming from
who knows where,
to do outlandish things
(while wide-eyed strangers stare)

to leap in front
of trains, pull emergency
chords, jump from tower
blocks, scream.
The compelling legacy
of dreams, perhaps, and
their mad imaginings.

Won't, of course,
despite the strong
mesmeric pull.
Too messy. Too final!

Besides, in the
queue other enticing
temptations brew.

To go two ways
down a one-way street
keep *on* the grass
not mind the doors

step on the cracks
of paving stones
ignore bad luck

tell a blonde
you know she's not –
duck!

at customs
declare your troubles,
faults, infidelities
(even your underwear)

stop when signs say go
run up the down escalator
embrace a nun
(what fun)
tweak a rabbi's beard
(how weird)

just once in a while,
in a fail-safe life, to dare
switch signposts round
make cars zoom
North
instead of
South

turn back Big Ben's
giant hands, delay
the News at Ten
make the nation wait
until *you* say when

ask a taxing taxi driver
for a tip, tell an unctuous
Maître d' his wine is off
that his haute cuisine
has turned you green

and when a stout
soprano shrills
(clearly over the hill!)
or a speech or turn
goes on too long and
interest palls, shout fire
clear the hall, have fun

not to cause mayhem
make them run
you understand, but just
to show one's flair
(because they're there)

irresistible at times –
almost – but of course
I never will.

Easier that way
I hear me say.

No Answer

It snowed the week you died.
An early spring blessing
some would say,
but I'd rather there'd been sun
to warm you on your way.

Earlier there was mud,
everywhere, then rain,
shovels at half tilt. Is this
a joke you've played on us?
Can we begin again?

There's no answer
from the telephone
no-one at the door.
However hard we call
we'll hear from you no more.

Ghosts and echoes fill the empty flat,
here the armchair where you always sat,
there the floppy hat you sometimes wore,
and in the dusty dressing table drawer
the fading pearls you kept for best.

It's cold, a window has been left ajar
and the evening breeze is snatching
at the curtain nets, petals spatter
the carpeted floor. Once full of song
this place is now an empty stage.
The piano waits, but the star has gone.

In Confidence

'This is to introduce a 70-year-old
gentleman', my GP wrote.
If it hadn't been me her clinical
note referred to, I might even
have been glad to meet him.
As it was, I wasn't.

I shouldn't have pried, of course,
she'd addressed it to the specialist,
not me, but at least I knew the score.
Charming and disarmingly young
as she was, she could have floored
me any time with her bedside manner.
Clearly I couldn't her, with mine.

The 'gentleman' was just about
palatable I guess, but as for
the rest, well hardly what you'd
call a tonic. Bad enough her
wanting me checked over 'just
in case', without this below-the-belt
blow to my masculine pride.
Doctors, it seems, should be treated
with care, strictly as prescribed.

Fortunately, it was all merely
precautionary and everything fine.
Still, not even the most skilled
of surgeons could, I fear, remove
my age, nor her pertinent words
from that tell-tale page.

Seems I'll just have to live with that,
or not, as the case may be, wait
another fifty years or so, and see.

Last Call

Messages can change your life,
and that one brought me
down to earth and nearly in it!

It wasn't what I expected,
needless to say, nor every day
you get an email asking if you're dead –
but get one I did, that stark winter
night, lightening splitting the sky
with true Shakespearean might.
The sender, his language blunt
and unambiguous, begged me
to respond with haste, assuring him
I wasn't – dead that is – and end his grief.
Far easier that way than if I were,
I thought, shrugging it off with
some relief. Clearly a prank,
no more, if in doubtful taste.

But no, it was for real.
Some faltering words on a nearby
phone brought the message home.
The anguished caller said he'd
heard I'd passed away (the euphemism
mine, not his). Would someone
please call back, inform him this
was wrong, he imploringly went on.
His deadly earnest voice
was tinged with funeral gloom.
It seemed the voice of doom.

Turning, I looked across the room
to see if I was there, but no, I was firmly
here, upright in my chair. I pinched
myself and all seemed well, stood
up, sat down, breathed deeply in
then out, poured myself a treble
scotch, felt my own pulse, picked
up the phone again. My name
was crystal clear for all to hear.
The word he used for dead was dead.
I felt like hell, my legs were lead.

Contemplating my near fate
I couldn't help but think how strange this was,
returning from the dead, not an angel,
not a devil in sight. An old Goon Show joke
ran wildly through my head – death must
be fun, nobody ever comes back:
thus the idiot voice of Eccles spoke.

The keyboard stared.
So tempting to answer as
my ghost, or simply put
Return to Sender and ping it back
rather than shock him with my
voice, though hard to resist that.
Perhaps I should offer him condolences,
he seemed so on the rack.

Even more tempting to hold fire
altogether, lie low, keep shtum,
supress my ire, seize this one-off
fallen-from-heaven chance to hear
the many extravagant things they'd
feel bound to say, read my own obituaries
if any, written by some kind friend
who pulled the shortest straw
(and kind they'd better be
for I'd be there behind his door!).

But then I thought again.
Did I really want my dear
ungrieving wife to be besieged
by all those tearful letters, sympathy
cards, calls – and then those po-faced,
top-hatted men in black, with their
frightening box, knocking at my door.
That would surely drop me to the floor!

So I picked up the phone and
slowly dialled. A cough, long pause,
much clearing of my throat. What
should I say? That this was me
calling from the other side,
that I hoped I wouldn't spoil his day?

No, my message back was clear.
Be of good cheer, high fives, I
was alive, and though I'd clearly
made him wait (he'd thrown
me into an almost terminal state),
the very last thing he could do now,
and never, ever again, was call me late.

Night after Night

I've been on many journeys of late,
often dangerous, sometimes alone,
sometimes with haunting figures from
the dead, or else with half-remembered
others who appear instead. Night after
night they blast my sleeping head,
filling me with dread.

And who is that beside me now
calling the shots? I know the face
but can't recall the name.
It's always the same.

Why are we speeding too close
to the cliff's edge – slam on the brakes!
Why are we adrift in this sky-high sea –
abandon ship, we're on the rocks,
the water's crashing in!

Who's waiting in that dark doorway,
who's that hooded by the kerb,
who's swinging that rusty chain?
My cover's blown, I'm on the run again.
There's a gun at my head.
I'm as good as dead.

There's a party raging round my bed,
the band's out of tune, their instruments grate.
I'm trapped in a surreal debate with people
I don't know in a language I don't speak.
Who are they all?
Whose voices these?
Why are they impossible to appease?

Just So

A dull man all his life
he jumped to fame at Chalk Farm
on an ordinary March morning
in a clerk-grey suit. Impulsive,
sick of the scrapings, of his
two drab semis (wife and home),
he threw himself, just so, without ado
beneath the eight thirty-two.

'Attention please', 'Attention please',
official voices brayed, proclaiming
the news to the waiting queues
at Colindale and Brent. And for thirty
time-is-money minutes, while passengers
cursed, were 'subject to some delay',
he was as good as there, in lights,
with Bank, with Waterloo,
a neon hero for a moment or two.

The Cartoonist's Glasses

for Peter Brookes

Borrowing his glasses to read the menu
I thought I'd get my own Private View,
that they'd reveal a flashlight world
of bloody tyrants and feckless politicians
where a pop-eyed prime minister and his
fellow schoolboy toffs held comic sway...
but all I saw was the dish of the day.

Of course it was his eyes I should have
borrowed, not his glasses, but they
weren't on offer as the wine was served,
his wit and wand hidden away in a
magician's cave, not yet ready to engage
and specially reserved – abracadabra –
for the next day's page.

The Seventh Day

'...and he rested on the seventh day from all he had done'.
Genesis 2.2

What is it, I wonder,
that draws me, a
non-observer, so
readily in, time upon
time, on Friday nights
as darkness falls?

It's not the prayers
you understand, not
the twisted chalah bread,
the wine, the candles.
Not simply these.

Nor even the ornate
silver cup that holds
the wine, the white cloth
covering the traditional
bread, embroidered round
the edge, the antique
candlesticks, the blessings over
this and that, the frayed black
book that guards the words
we say, its cover loose.

It's not just these, or not
only these, but the other precious
things they bring as well,

the friends and family with
us now, the family sadly gone
who prized and held all these
and passed them on.

It's also the Hebrew words
themselves (and not necessarily
what they mean), and this
timeless liturgy our forebears
clung to, even under regimes
that choked their liberty.

We do it all for all of them as well
as all of us, and bring them close.

And then, *Shabat Shalom* we say,
welcoming the Sabbath in, and hope
the peace the evening brings will stay.

Between You and Me

for my grandfather, Emanuel

Like sentinels we wheeled
you along paths, across fields
to a space beside a fence.
Everything you loathed was there:
grave clothes, grave countenances,

dull women in even duller hats,
the pomp and high-pitched
words you'd have topped
with a not-so-quiet aside.
Yet we were with you

all the way, your silent Tribe,
and when the clogs dropped
shattering the day, a bird flew
and something final snapped.
Moving on beyond the strangers'

stares, Shakespeare on my tongue,
Beethoven in my head, I knew
I'd find you there, not here,
amidst this black business.
One image sticks: a coffin

draped in a chandeliered hall,
mirrors uncovered, the usual
lights ablaze: to the left, poised,
a puzzled, watching bronze
and beside you, smiling down,

your favourite 'Dancing Girls'
their right legs raised.
As the service droned
I like to think you caught
their twinkling eyes, smiled
back true to form, winked.

Going Underground

The posters seem to be going up
as I ride the escalator down:
Legally Blonde: The Musical
vying with *Lucrezia Borgia,*
the opera; *Phantom,* the
Lloyd Webber, up against
War Horse and *A Flea in Your Ear.*

Strange bedfellows, strange
rivalries, but that's what brings
the fun – and sometimes pain –
life's quirky juxtaposings, with rivals
itching for the fight despite the
smiles they're often forced to feign.

Think of those thwarted thespians
up for an award, having to applaud
the bastards who pipped them
to the post, while cameras pan.
Those performances alone worthy
of an Oscar. Such guile, such ham!

Or Domingo and Pavarotti
high-fiving and smiling in the arena
while gaily topping each other's top C's.
Everyone getting their tenor's worth!
Even the gladiators of old would
have relished that titan clash...
and the cash.

And through history, so many juicy
rivalries. Cleopatra luring Anthony
to her bed, Wellington and Napoleon,
chests puffed, medals aglint, at
different ends of the cannons at Waterloo,
when only victory would do...
Churchill giving Hitler the ultimate V.
Allons enfants de la Patrie.

On occasion too, so-called sporting
rivalries seem to become battles
to the death as we cheer them on...
the quicksilver Ali versus the steam-
rolling Frasier, round after merciless
round in Manila, floating and stinging.
Both up when they should be
down, the ultimate thriller.

Or the effervescent McEnroe
and the ice-cool Borg peppering
the Wimbledon lawn, forever serving
for the set, or so it seemed.
Is either choking? You must be joking!

We've had our break points too,
you and I, on nights especially chilly,
me up when you are clearly down,
and often the reverse: the
perverse cross-fire of tetchy words
potentially as damaging as
cannon blast, fist, or blistering serve.

But being allies not rivals, in this
as in much more, we've never
had the need of fallible umpires –
or even Hawk-Eye – to watch and call
the score. Whenever danger's in sight
we've learned to grab the moving
hand rails, cling on tight.

The posters seem to be going
down now, as I ride swiftly up.

On Line

Steeped in the Torah,
immersed in the Koran,
at different ends of
the carriage, hardly a
heaven-sent marriage.

Whichever the prayer
whatever they do
at the very same time
they'll reach Waterloo.

But when it comes to vetting
by their own chosen God,
which one, I wonder,
will be getting the nod.

*

She's immersed in
Five Shades of Grey,
he in the *Sun*.
She won't look up,
he daren't look down.

*

She, quite a looker
is reading a book that's
just won the Booker,
he, behind his FT,
is dreaming up possible
ways he can hook her.

*

Once it was music *to* the ears
now its music, wham wham,
in the ears, and tweets to the
right of them texts to the left.
Back home, the end of a perfect
day, can they have anything
more to kindle, or say?

At the Grand Hotel, Cabourg

This resort has clearly seen better days.
It was here the young Marcel Proust
dunked a 'petite madeleine' in his tea,
recalling its particular taste for posterity.
And here he later spent long summers,
à la recherche, at the elegant Grand,
writing round the clock compulsively.

Meanwhile, oblivious, le tout Paris, in all
its finery, paced the promenade by day
like figures in a beachscape by Monet.

Now the once fashionable hotel, all
marble and chandeliers, seems to be
waiting for a ball to start. In the empty
dining room a lonely pianist plays a
Strauss waltz, keeping his own time.
An elderly couple, formally dressed, edge
gingerly towards closed veranda doors.

Outside, a fiery sea spray, flung by the
wind, coats the windows of empty cafés.
The adjacent casino, where roulette
wheels spun through long smoky nights
while orchestras swung and the great stars
of the day – Piaf, Chevalier, Trenet – held
sway, badly needs a coat of paint.

But I love it here for what it is, and was,
the tang of the giant waves, the voices in the air,
the departed cast somehow still there.

The hotel lights are ablaze now and
six floors up, on an ornate bedroom balcony
facing the sea, a girl and boy are kissing fervently.

What would Marcel have made of this, I wonder,
as he laboured to rekindle his lost years
behind drawn curtains in the room the hotel
now flaunts as his, only venturing down in the
early afternoon, when the coast was clear, for
his customary Sole Normande and a café au lait.

Summer will soon be here, and it won't be the
same, towels and deck chairs splaying the beech,
children splashing in the sea excitedly, the
exploding sound of balls on wooden bats.

I prefer it now, like this, out of season, when
the only voice you hear is his, and all you've
ever known or seen or done is here for company.

In an Elegiac Mood

for Michael Garrick

We were supposed to
jazz that night, but
you didn't show

and when we learned
you never would
we shuffled the music
and did what we could.

But though the numbers
all carried your name
and the sympathetic
audience cheered
it wasn't the same,
the chords on edge,
the rhythm tame.

We knew it wasn't
like you to miss a beat,
but your heartless
heart had done just that
and brought defeat.

And once the word
was out, the final credits
rolled and quickly grew,
so many fine compositions
in the queue.

You were supposed to be
there that night, at the piano,
driving the beat, leading
the way, but another
conductor trod on your
solos and stole the day.

That last chorus should
have been yours, not His,
and all the applause.

Note
On November 11, 2011, the day of a concert to mark 50 years of Poetry
and Jazz in Concert, for which he wrote and directed all the music, the
pianist and composer Michael Garrick was rushed into hospital for a
heart transplant. He died during the operation.

Last Night

for the jazz of MG

Last night was a night
of champagne and high kicking
and I strode that great hall
with a swaggering gait.
There were Liz, Kate, and Mary
in that raucous assembly,
and a Russian Princess
I had promised to take.

Yes, last night was a night
of fanfare and drum roll,
a cast of a thousand
all glitter and gold.
I watched them parading
like whores in the lamplight,
bejewelled and mascara'd
increasingly bold.

Then onto their necks
sprang the head of a monster,
instead of their laughter
shrieking and dread.
And into the room was
dragged a black coffin
and out of it stepped
a man long since dead

who greeted us all
with cheers and wild banter
embracing his wife,
his son, his black cat.
Then it all cut
to darkness and silence.
I woke up alone
the wrong end of the bed.

From the Top

One was called
Duke
the other Count
they were jazz's
royalty, they led
from the front.

And when
one... two... three
their pianos struck
the bass and drums
broke free
the saxophones
attacked
the raised horns
blazed back,
none could dispute
their sovereignty.

Lost for Words

I never quite know the words,
whether it's those rousing Last
Night of the Proms, Rule Britannia
Karaoke numbers the Promenaders
love to cheer and sing along to

or whether the potent psalms and
anthems I've known from ages past.
Somehow, however familiar, certain words
suddenly elude me, leaving me stranded
half way through, and God Save Our
something Queen just has to do!

Clearly, without me, there'll always
be an England, but nearer home,
when feelings swell, the caring words
of comfort, love, or hope that might
help wounded others cope somehow
arrive too late, or aren't quite right.

And even for you, the one who matters most,
whatever the praise, whatever the toast,
too often my litany of love falls short
as yet again my floundering words distort.

I never really know the words.

No Telling Why

There was no telling why: why
that office, why five twenty nine
that winter night, files shut,
dull eyes glued to the dawdling clock.
But come it did, and come to stay
it had: there was no coaxing it
from the long shelves to the rain
arrowing through the kerbside trees.

Its wings were tipped with white
its left foot ringed – not a phoenix
committing its ashes to the desert
wind, rising anew, but a pigeon,
prisoner in our earth-bound room.

Now a Nelson, gazing seaward, his
mind elsewhere, might turn a blind eye
to the birds, vying for peanuts at his
column's foot, spattering his Square,
but not we that bold intruder.

Frightened for it, by it, clumsily
with umbrellas, rulers, chairs
we stalked it, windows wide, sills
laced with bits of biscuit, bread.
Panicked, mistaking our intent,
it shot from side to side, rising
in plane bursts, making us dive.

It went, of course, at last,
leaving us dazed, in disarray,
each waiting the other's move,
none knowing quite why, having
strayed into our ordinary room,
it had wished to stay, why the room
itself had changed, why the city
night was spent now, blank, estranged.

Not Quite Right

They've just finished painting
the house we used to own,
and being that time of year
there's a wreath and holly
on the white wooden door.

We'd not have gone for that,
neither the brilliant white
nor the wreath, but a rather
warmer colour, and Chanukah
lights not a Christmas tree
in our old front room.
It doesn't feel quite right.

It's not my business now, for
sure, but it made me falter
just the same, strolling past
the other day, though it's
a number of years since
we moved away. There's
a lot of our life in there,
after all, a family growing up,
and memory stirs.

Of course, like gods and sin,
houses and colours have their
season, and which will last
and which will win, and what
the reason, is hard to say.
But I'd be opting for a
midnight blue, myself, and
Jehovah, if I had my way.

Offside

You're on my right
I'm on your left, you're
confused, you say.
At home it's clear –
me left, you right.
But here, in this bleak
room, this cold hotel,
all's in reverse...
and getting worse.
Above us, footsteps
pound a creaking floor.
A toilet flushes in
the room next door.

A woman's operatic
scream, startlingly near,
brings us to our feet,
ends all hope of sleep.
Someone's thundering
down the corridor.
It sounds like war.
Amber street lights,
swaying in the wind,
strafe the mottled walls.

Outside I'd like
to think a wolf was
baying at a moon
but no, there's just
a barking dog and the
traffic's throttled call.

We could of course
swap sides
tread familiar ground
or better still
meet in the middle
make sparks fly.

But not here,
not worth the try.
Angry pounding
on the wafer wall,
makes that clear.

A kind of sleep, a truce
of sorts, descends
at last – until a rap
like a cannon blast
shakes the flimsy door.
You should have put the
Don't Disturb sign up outside
you roar accusingly.
Our early-morning tea,
ordered the night before,
lies abandoned on the floor.
Nerves are raw. Clearly not
my day, or night, for sure.

Best admit defeat
retreat, drag our cases
down the narrow stairs.
The lift's out of order,
nobody cares.

Hopefully the car's
still where we left it late
last night, not clamped
or taken to the pound.
Surprise! Surprise!
It's nowhere to be found.
The last straw. Language
soars. It starts to rain.

But no, my fault again.
It's over here, to the right,
just as you despairingly
maintained, not over there,
behind that bus, as I
adamantly proclaimed.

In silence, fists tightly clenched,
drenched, we retrace our steps.
Too late to voice regrets.

A parking ticket, triumphant
on the window, smugly waits.
Yet another fine to pay!
I try to force a smile as foot
hard down we pull away.

Snapshots

I   Lauren

You were the first to land, just as
the first Allied bombs exploded on Iraq.
Not the kind of welcome or world
we'd have wished upon you.

Anxiously awaiting news in the hospital's
cold-white corridor, we took in the incandescent
TV screen and its grim communiqués.

The all-clear given at last by a reassuring nurse,
we were granted our first audience and sight
of a tiny you in your triumphant mother's arms.
Such innocence, I thought, puts us to shame.

It seemed only a blink away since your
mother and twin sister came our way
one miraculous September day, transforming
our lives. Impossible not to think back, but
forward too, and of what life might bring to you.

***

You grew towards us by the day, first this,
first that, word after enthralling word, every
child's miracle, and now almost nine years
along your exciting journey, and with two
young siblings on your tail, you're quite a girl.

Meanwhile, car-bombs, murder, famine, war
continue to augment their deadly score.
How long, I wonder, can the three of you
be shielded from this toxic brew.

Reading's your passion now – hours
locked in this book or that, shrugging
off your brother or sister's noisy
interventions, the great mystery of words
opening up their own mysterious worlds:
Harry Potter, *Swallows and Amazons*,
The Famous, timeless, *Five*.

The baby talk's long gone, and serious words
like 'regretfully', 'unfortunately', 'what if'
and 'but' punctuate your urgent sentences.
You sometimes frown as if a troubling
thought were weighing you down.

For all your serenity and style, your
natural sense of chic, your beguiling
smile, you're not above tripping
your brother dear or pinching his
arm when you think the coast is clear.
You love to sing, dance, dress up,
perform in plays, and though you're
through your ballerina phase, have sung
Over the Rainbow till you're blue, when
the X-Factor's on or they're picking a star
you'll perform it all vigorously anew, always
first, by far, to phone your vote through.

Secretly whispering to your friends, often
withdrawing of late into long silences,
you already have, it's clear, your own private
world and dreams we'll not be party to,
and rightly so. Your time will quickly come
and ours, even more quickly, go.

II   Sam

Dearest Sam, you always were our
dangerman, swinging Tarzan-like
from things not made to swing from,
leaping from ledges too high, touching ovens
too hot, vases too breakable, opening,
turning, pulling everything in sight,
keeping us all in a constant state of fright.

And when, on red alert, we
try to rein you in, protect you
from yourself with warning shouts,
you come back with the same
Why, Why, Why refrain, again and again,
like a needle stuck in the grooves
of those old LPs we used to play
on rainy Sunday afternoons.

It's all change now, or almost so.
I'm glad to say the cricket bat you
proudly swing now meets the ball
and not your sisters' heads, and when
you bowl, the ball is mainly aimed
directly at the stumps instead.

Yet racing down corridors, practicing
karate kicks in the kitchen, you're still
our dangerman, and if there's a wall or
window to bang into, you will surely bang.
But those Sam missiles seem
to be detonated with more care
these days, the fallout rare.

With your sisters taunting you
on either side you have to take
a manly stand from time to time.
I understand. (We exchange
knowing winks from behind our hands
conspiringly, man to man).

You still throw questions galore,
but sharper and more searching than
before, now clearly aimed at learning more.
In time, I fear, the answers may
not be ours to give, something
we hope you will eventually forgive.

The word from school is that your
teachers find you bright, cute looking,
the ladies say, sensitive, even quiet!
They're right. It won't be long before
those gentle eyes are putting girls to flight
with not a 'why' or broken spring in sight.

III   Caitlin

You follow in the others' wake,
all two foot something of you,
and there's not the gale will
make you trim your sail.

An all-laughing, all-go
anything-they-can-do-I-can-do
cuddly star is what you are.
No swing's too high, slope
too steep, jump too far.
An oasis of endless fun
you keep us on the run.

And even when the others push,
trip you up, pull your pigtail
or take your space, your ever-
ready smile remains in place.
You've only just turned four
but are always back for more.

You know all the steps, all the tunes,
join their chorus with great glee,
and even if you can't quite get the words
you just make up your own,
quite undeterred, hilariously.

You spin around us like a top.
May you never stop.

January 2012

Anniversary

Opening the batting in those junior
school years, how I dreamt of
carrying my bat, scoring an heroic
hundred, or even getting a fiery
fifty on the board. It never came to
that, of course. Too many catches
edged to the preying slips or looped
to some grasping fielder on the boundary.
All those gruelling evenings in the nets
('attack', 'defend') brought little dividend.

But now, amazingly, there's another
kind of fifty on the board, though it
seems a myth. Aren't we just walking
to the crease, you and I, taking careful
guard, about to hit them all for six?

We've needed luck, of course,
nearly ran ourselves out on more
than one occasion, but so far,
mercifully, the third umpire has
looked the other way. Besides,
there's more than mere runs up
there now, and a strong family team
all padded-up to follow us in.

The freshly painted sight screens
may no longer shield the view as
determined bowlers race in on cue.
And while we know we'll never see
this hundred up we'll still play every ball,
block, duck, continue to eke the runs out
one by one as we have always done, as if
this were a match that could still be won.

Acknowledgements

My particular thanks to Andy Croft, whose Smokestack Books is a beacon of light in the misty world of contemporary publishing – also to my wife Carole, and to our daughters Manuela and Deborah. Thanks also to the BBC and to the editors of the various journals and papers where some of these poems first appeared.

JR